This book belongs to:

. . . .

Mrs Wordsmith®

FIRST GRADE ENGLISH

GARGANTUAN WORKBOOK

Bearnice

Bogart

Brick

Plato

Grit

Yin & Yang

Armie

Shang High

Oz

MEET THE
CHARACTERS

CONTENTS

PHONICS & PHONOLOGICAL AWARENESS

can you say?

ai

paint

AI
upper case

ai
lower case

Vowel sounds can be long or short. Long vowels can be made with a single letter or a digraph (two letters making one sound).

The sound of **a** in **apple** is a short vowel sound. The sound of **ai** in **paint** is a long vowel sound.

FIND IT

Can you find the letters for the **ai** sound that are in the words in bold? Circle them.

Plato **painted** a **portrait** with his **tail**.

1. Read each sound.
   Read each sound again
   faster. Read the sounds
   together smoothly.

2. Trace the dotted letter.
   Follow Bogart's emoji.

3. Trace and write the letters.

POWER UPS

Blend the letters
to read the words.

sail   **tail**   **rain**

can you say?

ee

seek

EE
upper case

ee
lower case

Can you find the letters for the **ee** sound that are in the words in bold? Circle them.

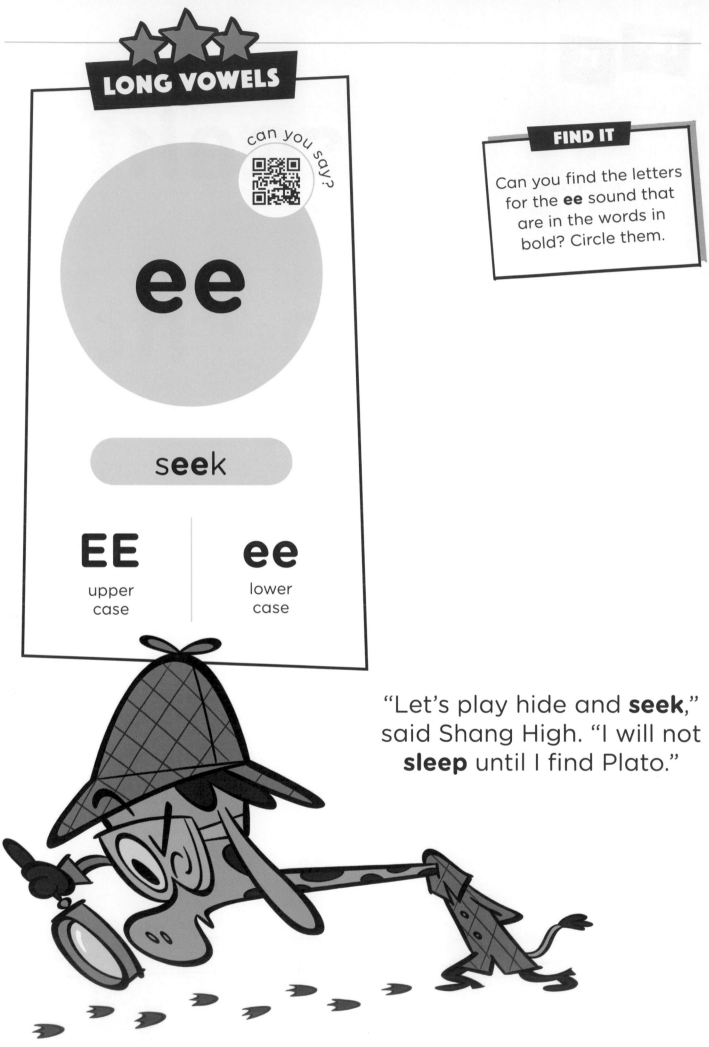

"Let's play hide and **seek**," said Shang High. "I will not **sleep** until I find Plato."

1. Read each sound.
   Read each sound again
   faster. Read the sounds
   together smoothly.

2. Trace the dotted letter.
   Follow Bogart's emoji.

3. Trace and write the letters.

POWER UPS

Blend the letters
to read the words.

queen   bee   sheep

can you say?

igh

fight

IGH
upper case

igh goes in the middle or at the end of the word

Can you find the letters for the **igh** sound that are in the words in bold? Circle them.

"I will **fight** for the treasure with all my **might**!"

fight

1. Read each sound.
   Read each sound again
   faster. Read the sounds
   together smoothly.

2. Trace the dotted letter.
   Follow Bogart's emoji.

3. Trace and write the letters.

POWER UPS

Blend the letters
to read the words.

right   night   high

can you say?

oa

soak

OA	oa
upper case	lower case

Can you find the letters for the **oa** sound that are in the words in bold? Circle them.

Bearnice **soaked** her hair in **soapy** water.

1. Read each sound.
   Read each sound again
   faster. Read the sounds
   together smoothly.

2. Trace the dotted letter.
   Follow Bogart's emoji.

3. Trace and write the letters.

POWER UPS

Blend the letters
to read the words.

boat   road   soap

can you say?

oo

shampoo

OO
upper case

oo goes in the middle or at the end of the word

Can you find the letters for the oo sound that are in the words in bold? Circle them.

"Oops!"

Bearnice put **too** much **shampoo** in her hair!

1. Read each sound.
   Read each sound again
   faster. Read the sounds
   together smoothly.

shampoo

2. Trace the dotted letter.
   Follow Bogart's emoji.

shampoo

3. Trace and write the letters.

POWER UPS

Blend the letters
to read the words.

too   food   room

VOWEL SOUNDS

SHORT VOWELS

a cat

e bed

i fish

o sock

u sun

LONG VOWELS

ai rain

ee feet

igh night

oa boat

oo boot

FIND THE VOWEL

Is the vowel long or short?
Write **S** in the box if the vowel is short.
Write **L** in the box if the vowel is long.

rain [L]

cat [ ]

paint [ ]

egg [ ]

feet [ ]

bed [ ]

night [ ]

pig [ ]

milk [ ]

mop [ ]

goat [ ]

boat [ ]

duck [ ]

boot [ ]

sun [ ]

19

SHORT OR LONG VOWEL A

Vowel sounds can be long or short. Long vowels can be made with a single letter or a digraph (two letters making one sound).

The sound of **a** in **apple** is a short vowel sound. The sound of **ai** in **rain** is a long vowel sound.

First, choose the correct word to match to the image.
Next, circle **S** if the vowel is **short** or circle **L** if the vowel is **long**.

cat | paint | ant | rain

1.

paint

S | (L)

2.

S | L

3.

S | L

4.

S | L

SHORT OR LONG VOWEL E

The sound of **e** in **bed** is a short vowel sound.
The sound of **ee** in **green** is a long vowel sound.

red | feet | sheep | nest

1.

sheep

S | (L)

2.

S | L

3.

S | L

4.

S | L

Vowel sounds can be long or short. Long vowels can be made with a single letter or a digraph (two letters making one sound).

The sound of **i** in **big** is a short vowel sound. The sound of **igh** in **fight** is a long vowel sound.

First, choose the correct word to match to the image.
Next, circle **S** if the vowel is **short** or circle **L** if the vowel is **long**.

light | ring | night | fish

1.

fish

Ⓢ | L

2.

S | L

3.

S | L

4.

S | L

SHORT OR LONG VOWEL O

The sound of **o** in **mop** is a short vowel sound.
The sound of **oa** in **soap** is a long vowel sound.

| toast | toad | box | dog |

1.

toad

S | **L**

2.

S | L

3.

S | L

4.

S | L

SHORT OR LONG VOWEL U

Vowel sounds can be long or short. Long vowels can be made with a single letter or a digraph (two letters making one sound).

The sound of **u** in **tub** is a short vowel sound.
The sound of **oo** in **boot** is a long vowel sound.

First, choose the correct word to match to the image.
Next, circle **S** if the vowel is **short** or circle **L** if the vowel is **long**.

| sun | shampoo | food | bug |

1.

sun

(S) | L

2.

_____

S | L

3.

_____

S | L

4.

_____

S | L

SORT THE SHORT & LONG VOWEL WORDS

Sort out the short and long vowel words. Write the short vowel words on the left and long vowel words on the right.

SORT THE WORDS

bag   soap   room   milk   frog

high   ant   sail   sun   bee

SHORT VOWEL WORDS

bag

_____

_____

_____

_____

LONG VOWEL WORDS

_____

_____

_____

_____

_____

can you say?

oo

book

OO
upper case

Remember! The same grapheme (letter or letters) can represent more than one sound.

Can you find the letters for the **oo** sound that are in the words in bold? Circle them.

Armie **took** his time. He **looked** carefully at every picture in the **book**.

book

1. Read each sound.
   Read each sound again
   faster. Read the sounds
   together smoothly.

2. Trace the dotted letter.
   Follow Bogart's emoji.

3. Trace and write the letters.

POWER UPS

Blend the letters
to read the words.

look   good   took

27

can you say?

ar

alarm

AR	**ar**
upper case	lower case

Grit couldn't move his **arm** to turn off the **large alarm**.

1. Read each sound. Read each sound again faster. Read the sounds together smoothly.

2. Trace the dotted letter. Follow Bogart's emoji.

3. Trace and write the letters.

POWER UPS

Blend the letters to read the words.

car   **part**   **bark**

can you say?

or

sport

OR

upper case

or

lower case

Can you find the letters for the **or** sound that are in the words in bold? Circle them.

Oz was good at every **sport**.

1. Read each sound.
   Read each sound again
   faster. Read the sounds
   together smoothly.

sport

2. Trace the dotted letter.
   Follow Bogart's emoji.

sport

3. Trace and write the letters.

POWER UPS

Blend the letters
to read the words.

born   fork   cord

can you say?

ur

surf

UR
upper case

ur
lower case

FIND IT

Can you find the letters for the **ur** sound that are in the words in bold? Circle them.

Brick loved to **surf** with the **turtles** and the fish.

1. Read each sound.
   Read each sound again
   faster. Read the sounds
   together smoothly.

2. Trace the dotted letter.
   Follow Bogart's emoji.

3. Trace and write the letters.

POWER UPS

Blend the letters
to read the words.

burn   curl   fur

can you say?

ow

howl

OW
upper case

ow
lower case

Can you find the letters for the **ow** sound that are in the words in bold? Circle them.

Plato always **howls** when the **shower** is full **power**.

1. Read each sound.
   Read each sound again
   faster. Read the sounds
   together smoothly.

2. Trace the dotted letter.
   Follow Bogart's emoji.

3. Trace and write the letters.

POWER UPS

Blend the letters
to read the words.

cow   down   now

SORT THE SHORT & LONG VOWEL WORDS

Sort out the short and long vowel words. Write the short vowel words on the left and long vowel words on the right.

SORT THE WORDS

map   hat   feet   coin   night

man   plum   tree   duck   join

SHORT VOWEL WORDS

map

LONG VOWEL WORDS

SORT THE WORDS

hot mop point moon stuck
tooth queen tail cap kit

SHORT VOWEL WORDS

hot

LONG VOWEL WORDS

can you say?

oi

coin

OI
upper case

oi
lower case

FIND IT

Can you find the letters for the **oi** sound that are in the words in bold? Circle them.

Armie **pointed** at the **coins** and said, "Let's count them."

38

1. Read each sound.
   Read each sound again
   faster. Read the sounds
   together smoothly.

2. Trace the dotted letter.
   Follow Bogart's emoji.

3. Trace and write the letters.

POWER UPS

Blend the letters
to read the words.

join   point

39

can you say?

ear

fear

EAR	**ear**
upper case	lower case

Can you find the letters for the **ear** sound that are in the words in bold? Circle them.

She jumped with **fear** when a spider **appeared**.

1. Read each sound.
   Read each sound again
   faster. Read the sounds
   together smoothly.

2. Trace the dotted letter.
   Follow Bogart's emoji.

3. Trace and write the letters.

POWER UPS

Blend the letters
to read the words.

ear   hear   year

LONG VOWELS

air

can you say?

hair

AIR	**air**
upper case	lower case

FIND IT

Can you find the letters for the **air** sound that are in the words in bold? Circle them.

"It's not **fair**!" grumbled Grit.

"I hate brushing my **hair**."

42

1. Read each sound.
   Read each sound again
   faster. Read the sounds
   together smoothly.

2. Trace the dotted letter.
   Follow Bogart's emoji.

3. Trace and write the letters.

POWER UPS

Blend the letters
to read the words.

pair **chair** **fair**

can you say?

ure

cure

URE

upper case

ure goes in the middle or at the end of the word

Can you find the letters for the **ure** sound that are in the words in bold? Circle them.

"I've found the **cure**!" cried Armie.

TRY IT

1. Read each sound.
   Read each sound again
   faster. Read the sounds
   together smoothly.

cure

2. Trace the dotted letter.
   Follow Bogart's emoji.

3. Trace and write the letters.

POWER UPS

Blend the letters
to read the words.

sure   **pure**   **lure**

can you say?

er

mermaid

ER	er
upper case	lower case

"A **mermaid** is part **person**, part fish," explained Plato.

46

1. Read each sound.
   Read each sound again
   faster. Read the sounds
   together smoothly.

mermaid

2. Trace the dotted letter.
   Follow Bogart's emoji.

mermaid

3. Trace and write the letters.

POWER UPS

Blend the letters
to read the words.

her   boxer   herb

LONG
VOWEL CHART

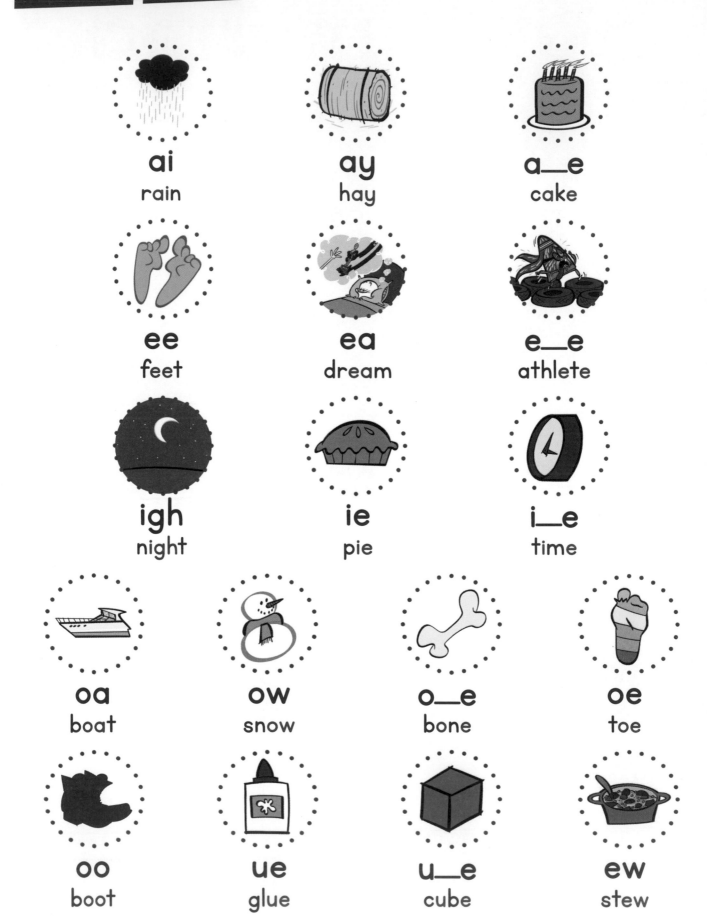

ai
rain

ay
hay

a__e
cake

ee
feet

ea
dream

e__e
athlete

igh
night

ie
pie

i__e
time

oa
boat

ow
snow

o__e
bone

oe
toe

oo
boot

ue
glue

u__e
cube

ew
stew

LONG VOWELS: ADDING e

Write out these words, add **e**, and see how the pronunciation and meaning changes.

Draw a curved line to show the two letters making the long vowel sound.

1.

cap   cape

2.

can

LONG VOWELS: ADDING e

Adding e can turn a short vowel into a long vowel.

3.

kit

_____

4.

rob

_____

50

Write out these words, add **e**, and see how the pronunciation and meaning changes.

Draw a curved line to show the two letters making the long vowel sound.

5. **cub**	-------------------------------
6. **tap**	-------------------------------
7. **cut**	-------------------------------
8. **hat**	-------------------------------

Two vowels can work together as a vowel team. This is called a digraph, when two letters make a single sound.

Underline the vowel team and then circle the picture that matches the word.

1. t**oa**d

 **OR**

2. **beach**

 **OR**

The first vowel in the team is bold.
It says its name, making a long vowel sound.
The second vowel in the team is shy. It stays silent.

3. **sail**

 **OR**

4. **coat**

 **OR**

Underline the vowel team and then
circle the picture that matches the word.

5. **sweet**

 **OR**

6. **peas**

 **OR**

LONG VOWELS: COMPLETE THE WORDS

Sleepy Shang High spilled vowel teams all over the floor.

Help him clean up by completing the words.

1.

emai**l**

 | **ea**

2.

b _____

ee | oa

3.

wh _____ **l**

oa | ee

4.

b _____ **t**

ai | oa

LONG VOWELS: COMPLETE THE WORDS

Sleepy Shang High spilled vowel teams all over the floor.

Help him clean up by completing the words:

5.

br____n

ai | ee

6.

r____d

ea | ai

7.

g____t

ue | oa

8.

t____

ie | oa

SAME LONG VOWEL SOUNDS

oi and **oy** are different spellings that make the same vowel sound

oi
c**oi**n

oi is often used at the
beginning or **middle** of a word

oy
t**oy**

oy is often used at the
end of a word

ow and **ou** are different spellings that make the same vowel sound

ou
h**ou**se

ou is often used at the
beginning or **middle** of a word

ow
c**ow**

ow is used at the **beginning**,
middle, or **end** of a word

Complete the word!

1. **toy**

(oy) | ou

2. s____l

ow | oi

3. j____

ow | oy

4. t____let

oi | ow

Complete the word!

5. **h** _____ **l**

ow | oi

6. **cl** _____ **d**

ou | oi

7. _____ **l**

oy | ow

8. **fl** _____ **er**

ow | oy

SAME LONG VOWEL SOUNDS

Complete the word!

9. **sn** _____

ow | ou

10. **b** _____ **l**

oy | oi

11. **m** _____ **se**

ow | ou

12. **ann** _____

oy | oi

R-CONTROLLED VOWELS

Many long vowels have an **r** in them. These are sometimes called r-controlled vowels.

er, **ir**, and **ur** are different spellings that often make the same sound.

er
germ

ir
bird

ur
surf

ar and **or** make their own sounds.

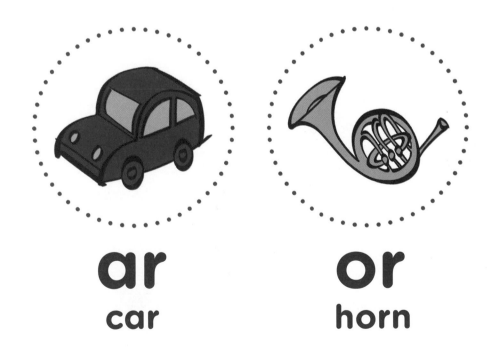

ar
car

or
horn

Yin and Yang go to a party!
They make lots of friends!

Help Yin and Yang describe their new friends.

Circle the word that best matches the picture.

1. **nurse** | **curl**

2. **shark** | **farm**

3. **girl** | **thirsty**

4. **hurt** | **turkey**

5. **turtle** | **slurp**

6. **herd** | **germs**

Oz wrote a list of everything
she wants for her birthday.

But some of the letters are missing!

Complete the words to match the pictures.

1.

j a r

(ar) | er

2.

h _____ se

ur | or

3.

b _____ ger

ar | ur

4.

popc _____ n

or | ar

5.

sh _____ t

ir | or

6.

_____ t

ar | ur

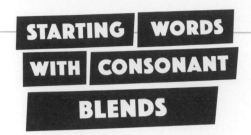

STARTING WORDS WITH CONSONANT BLENDS

Consonant blends are two consonants that are next to each other in a word. This can make them harder to sound out and spell.

Sometimes these letters are called adjacent consonants. You say each consonant quickly, so their sounds blend together.

Help Brick and Yang make an epic consonant blend smoothie!

Complete the word with a consonant blend to match the picture.

1.

_____**crab**

dr **cr** **gr**

2.

_____**ock**

cl **fl** **m**

64

3.

_____ **anet**

pl   sn   br

4.

_____ **arf**

sp   tw   sc

5.

_____ **airs**

st   br   tw

6.

_____ **ower**

fl   pl   tr

7.

_____ **ake**

tw   fl   sn

8.

_____ **ess**

dr   gr   sk

Consonant blends are two consonants that are next to each other in a word. This can make them harder to sound out and spell.

Sometimes these letters are called adjacent consonants. You say each consonant quickly, so their sounds blend together.

Oz is making a movie! Help her choose which props to use.

Circle the word that matches the picture.

Underline the starting consonant blend.

1.

(swing) or **frog**

2.

stop or **star**

66

3.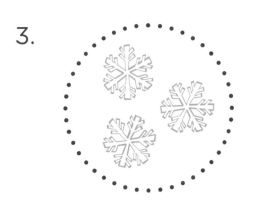

snow or **spin**

4.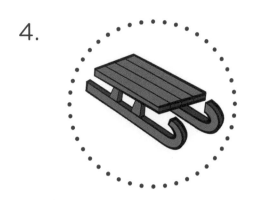

sleep or **sled**

5.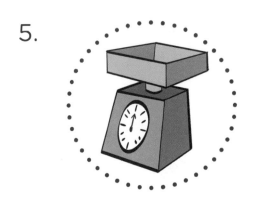

skate or **scale**

6.

frown or **crown**

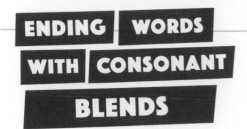

ENDING WORDS WITH CONSONANT BLENDS

Consonant blends are two consonants that are next to each other in a word. This can make them harder to sound out and spell.

Sometimes these letters are called adjacent consonants. You say each consonant quickly, so their sounds blend together.

Help Brick and Yang make an epic consonant blend smoothie!

Complete the word with a consonant blend to match the picture.

1.

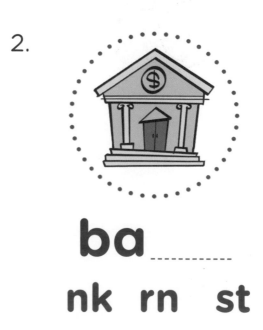

po nd

mp (nd) st

2.

ba_____

nk   rn   st

68

3.

pai_____

lk   nt   ft

4.

toa_____

rm   nd   st

5.

la_____

mp   rf   nk

6.

ne_____

st   ld   nk

7.

e_____

ct   lf   fr

8.

ha_____

rt   rk   nd

Consonant blends are two consonants that are next to each other in a word. This can make them harder to sound out and spell.

Sometimes these letters are called adjacent consonants. You say each consonant quickly, so their sounds blend together.

Oz is making a movie! Help her choose which props to use.

Circle the word that matches the picture.

Underline the ending consonant blend.

1.

(stamp) or **sink**

2.

sand or **band**

3.

test or **tent**

4.

golf or **gold**

5.

lift or **gift**

6.

toast or **boast**

Words are made up of sounds. Some words end with the same sounds. These words rhyme.

Circle the picture that rhymes with the word.

1. **sing**

2. **fell**

4. **wall**

3. **rock**

5. **look**

Circle the word that does not rhyme with the other words.

1.   **three**   **tree**   (**wash**)

2.   **red**   **bag**   **bed**

3.   **pot**   **sun**   **fun**

4.   **bug**   **star**   **mug**

5.   **fish**   **dish**   **lock**

Words are made up of sounds. Some words end with the same sounds. These words rhyme.

Complete the poem with the word that rhymes.

Row, row, row your boat, gently down the stream.

If you see a crocodile, don't forget to _____!

shout   **scream**

Three little monkeys
jumping on the bed,

One fell down and
bumped
his _____.

head   foot

Mama called the
doctor and the
doctor said,

"No more monkeys
jumping on
the _____!"

grass   bed

ang, ing, ong, ung!

Big Ben is broken! It goes "ang ing ong ung!"

Sometimes, you have to remember to say the letters at the end of a word differently. You say all the letter sounds, but in a faster and stickier way, like ang, ing, ong, and ung. These are sometimes called glued sounds.

Underline the glued endings. Circle the word that matches the picture.

1.

(ring) | sung

2.
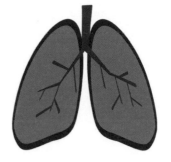
lung | wrong

3.

hang | sing

4.

fang | king

76

5.

wing | thing

6.

long | dung

7.

gong | swing

8.

song | bang

9.

sting | bring

10.

strong | string

PHONICS:
SOUND BUTTONS & READING PRACTICE

1. Sound button the words.

When a single letter (grapheme) makes one sound (phoneme), put a **dot** under it.

cat

Spot the vowel teams or consonant teams and **underline** them.

night   tail   chat

2. Blend and read the words.

1.	**feel**	2.	**book**
3.	**rain**	4.	**night**
5.	**feet**	6.	**tool**
7.	**near**	8.	**wail**

9. **soak**   10. **look**

11. **sail**   12. **right**

13. **moon**   14. **boat**

15. **fight**   16. **seem**

Try to decode these nonreal words in the same way.

17. **zook**   18. **naim**

19. **beem**   20. **jight**

PHONICS:
SOUND BUTTONS &
READING PRACTICE

1. Sound button the words.

When a single letter (grapheme) makes one sound (phoneme), put a **dot** under it.

cat
• • •

Spot the vowel teams or consonant teams and **underline** them.

night   **tail**   **chat**

2. Blend and read the words.

3. Real or not real?

On this page, there are words that are real and words that are not real. You have to decide which is which.

Check the box if the word is **real**.

cat ✓   **pag** ☐
• • •   • • •

---

1. **gilk** ☐

2. **clap** ☐

3. **bleed** ☐

4. **spait** ☐

5. **freeg** ☐

6. **pump** ☐

7. **coach** ☐   8. **crab** ☐

9. **float** ☐   10. **rant** ☐

11. **sand** ☐   12. **list** ☐

13. **throat** ☐   14. **bink** ☐

15. **truck** ☐   16. **lift** ☐

17. **creek** ☐   18. **deed** ☐

PHONICS:
SOUND BUTTONS &
READING PRACTICE

INSTRUCTIONS:

1. Sound button the words.

When a single letter (grapheme) makes one sound (phoneme), put a **dot** under it.

cat
· · ·

Spot the vowel teams or consonant teams and **underline** them.

night   tail   chat

2. Blend and read the words.

1.   **insect**

2.   **invent**

3.   **sleeping**

4.   **napkin**

5.   **painting**

6.   **sickness**

82

7. **fishing**

8. **backpack**

9. **feeling**

10. **airbus**

11. **darkness**

12. **unless**

13. **family**

14. **habit**

Try to decode these nonreal words in the same way.

15. **femely**

16. **exun**

17. **ganrock**

18. **grinit**

PHONICS:
SOUND BUTTONS & READING PRACTICE

INSTRUCTIONS:

1. Sound button the words.

When a single letter (grapheme) makes one sound (phoneme), put a **dot** under it.

cat
• • •

Spot the vowel teams or consonant teams and **underline** them.

night   tail   chat
• ▬ • ▬   • ▬ •   ▬ • •

Spot the vowel teams with final **-e** (split digraphs) and connect them.

cake
• ‿ ◡

2. Blend and read the words.

3. Real or not real?

On this page, there are words that are real and words that are not real. You have to decide which is which.

Check the box if the word is **real**.

cat ✓   pag ☐
• • •   • • •

1. **herb** ☐   2. **germ** ☐

3. **star** ☐   4. **whuck** ☐

5. **glane** ☐   6. **care** ☐

7. **gife** ☐

8. **dare** ☐

9. **key** ☐

10. **more** ☐

11. **feal** ☐

12. **roink** ☐

13. **slow** ☐

14. **shake** ☐

15. **bird** ☐

16. **bark** ☐

17. **term** ☐

18. **lie** ☐

PHONICS:
SOUND BUTTONS &
READING PRACTICE

1. Sound button the words.

When a single letter (grapheme) makes one sound (phoneme), put a **dot** under it.

cat

Spot the vowel teams or consonant teams and **underline** them.

night **tail** **chat**

Spot the vowel teams with final **-e** (split digraphs) and connect them.

cake

2. Blend and read the words.

Remember to blend and read each syllable first and then the whole word.

1. **athlete**

2. **needy**

3. **messy**

4. **delete**

5. **meeting**

6. **cheeky**

7. **sleepy**

8. **complete**

9. **songbird**

10. **flying**

11. **dirty**

12. **thirteen**

13. **fairly**

14. **concrete**

Try to decode these nonreal words in the same way.

15. **keady**

16. **reedful**

17. **greeming**

18. **coateen**

VOCABULARY

BIG & SMALL

A synonym is a word that means the same as another word. These are synonyms of big.

These mean big; very big; and very, very big.

enormous
gargantuan
colossal

huge
giant

big

An antonym is a word that means the opposite of another word. These are antonyms of big.

These mean small; very small; and very, very small.

small

tiny

minuscule
microscopic

VOCABULARY

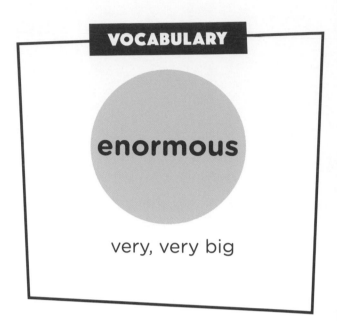

enormous

very, very big

Circle the words that mean the same as **big**.

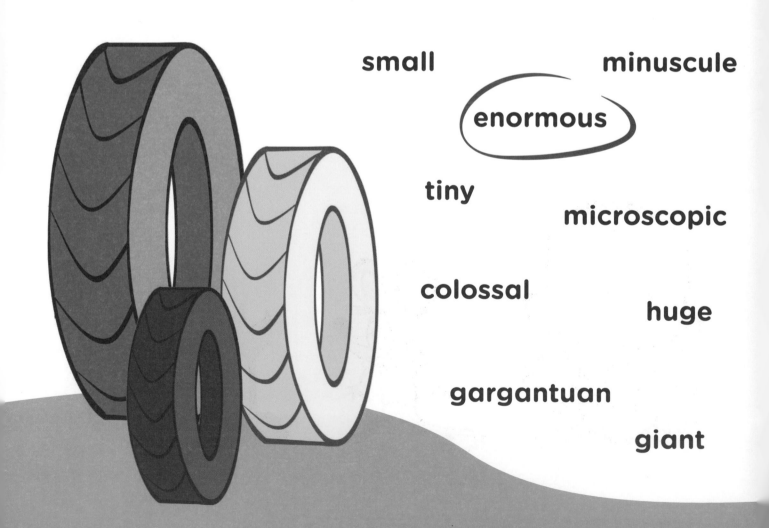

small   minuscule

(enormous)

tiny

microscopic

colossal

huge

gargantuan

giant

HAPPY & SAD

A synonym is a word that means the same as another word. These are synonyms of happy.

These mean happy; very happy; and very, very happy.

happy **delighted** **overjoyed**
ecstatic

An antonym is a word that means the opposite of another word. These are antonyms of happy.

These mean sad; very sad; and very, very sad.

sad

upset
melancholy

heartbroken

ecstatic

very, very happy

Circle the words that mean the same as **happy**.

delighted   melancholy

upset

heartbroken

overjoyed

sad

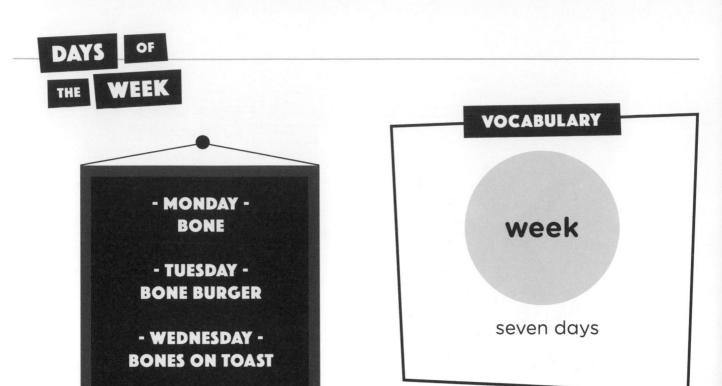

- MONDAY -
BONE

- TUESDAY -
BONE BURGER

- WEDNESDAY -
BONES ON TOAST

VOCABULARY

week

seven days

Look at the specials board and write the correct days of the week in the blanks!

1. Monday

2. ....

3. ....

- THURSDAY -
CHICKENLESS BONE
BUCKET

- FRIDAY -
SUPERSIZE BONE

- SATURDAY -
BONE CONE

- SUNDAY -
BASIC BONE BROTH

4.

Thursday

5.

6.

7.

MONTHS OF THE YEAR

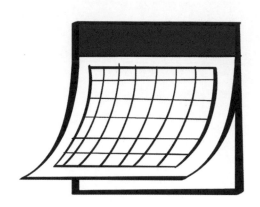

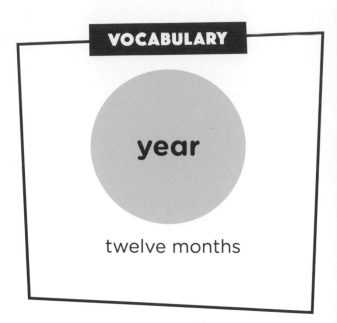

VOCABULARY

year

twelve months

Choose the correct months of the year and write them in the blanks!

January

F _____

M _____

A _____

M _____

J _____

98

June	October	August
September	April	February
May	January	March
November	December	July

J u l y _____

A _____

S _____

O _____

N _____

D _____

PUT THE WORDS IN ALPHABETICAL ORDER

Grit is opening an ice cream shop!
Help him design his dream menu.

Put the words below in alphabetical order. This means put them
in the order that their first letters appear in the alphabet.

strawberry   **mint**   **lemon**   **coconut**

orange   **blueberry**   **grape**   **vanilla**

1. blueberry   2. _____   3. _____

4. _____   5. _____   6. _____

7. _____   8. _____

Uh oh... there has been a messy mistake!
There's paint everywhere!

Help the characters clean up by naming all the paints.

**blue | red | green | purple
yellow | white | pink**

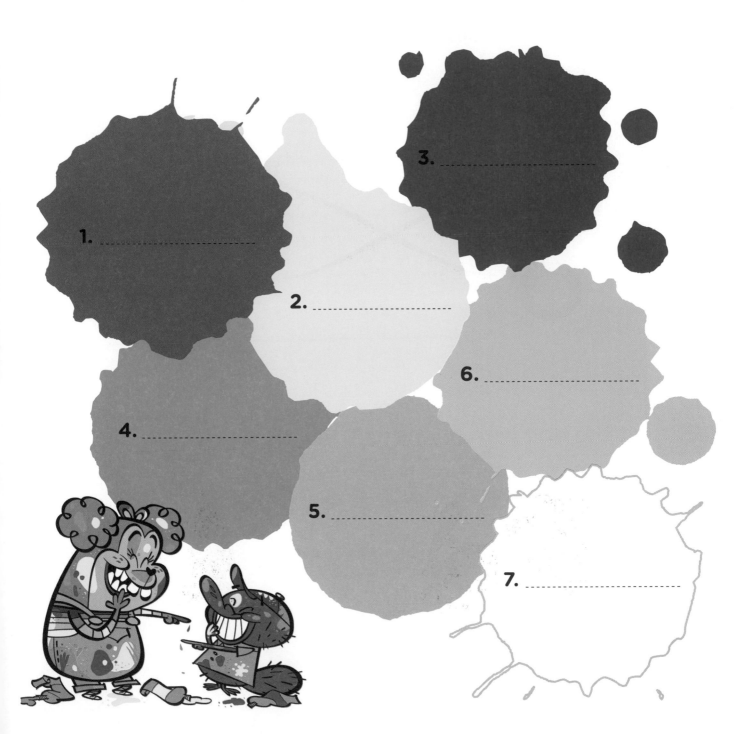

1. _____

2. _____

3. _____

4. _____

5. _____

6. _____

7. _____

Some words look the same but have different meanings. Bark is the noise that dogs make and the outside part of a tree.

Match the sentences to the pictures.
Draw a line to connect them.

1. The bells ring.   She is wearing a ring.

2. I hit the ball with my bat.   The bat can fly.

3. He is a fan of sports!   The fan kept them cool.

4. He has a cold.   It is cold outside.

5. She waves with both arms.   The ocean waves are strong.

GRAMMAR

VOCABULARY

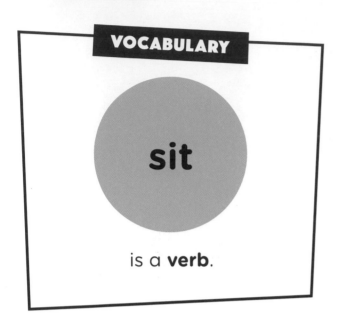

sit

is a **verb**.

A verb is all about doing or being.
Often, they are action words like sit, eat, and laugh.

Circle the verbs on this page!

jump

sit

hairy

lemon

be

think

magnet

draw

taste

106

VOCABULARY

scarf

is a **noun**.

A noun is a person, place, or thing,
like Armie, Earth, and scarf.

Circle the nouns on this page!

scarf

tree

little

Oz

paint

house

tired

yellow

beach

107

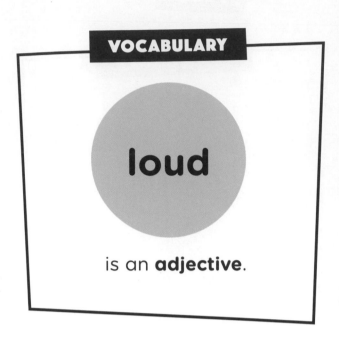

loud

is an **adjective**.

An adjective is a describing word.
It describes a noun, like <u>loud</u> music.

Circle the adjectives on this page!

quiet

loud

ball

carrot

swim

tired

blue

hot

frozen

ACTION VERBS

An action verb is a verb that describes an action,
like run or smile.

Choose the action verb that best describes the picture. Write the verbs in the blanks.

ACTION WORDS

1. _____ Swim _____

2. _____

3. _____

4. _____

sleep

read

kick

swim

109

Prepositions tell you where something
is or where something happens.

Write the prepositions next to the matching picture.

1.

- -

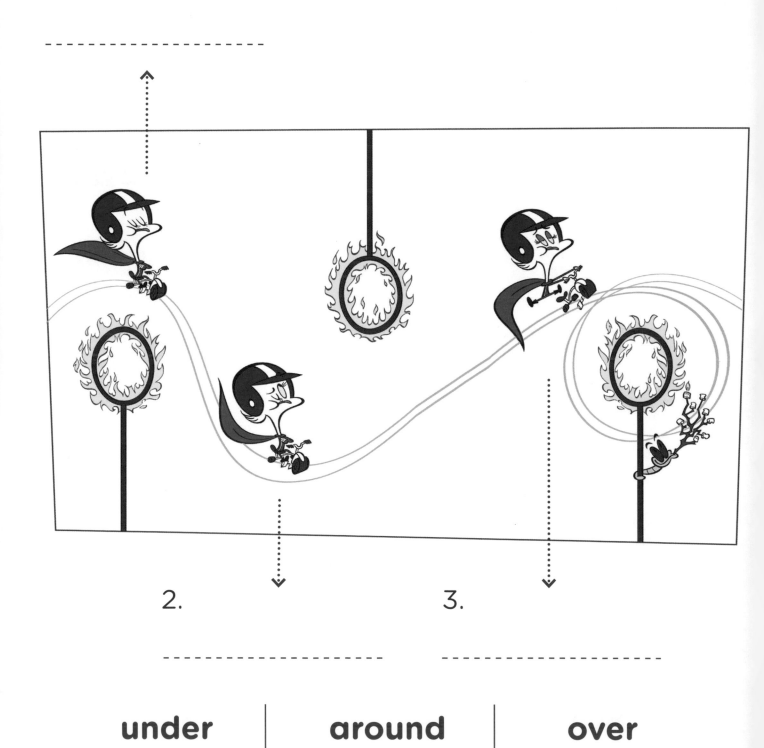

2.

3.

- - - - - - - - - - - - - - - - - -   - - - - - - - - - - - - - - - - - -

under | **around** | **over**

4.

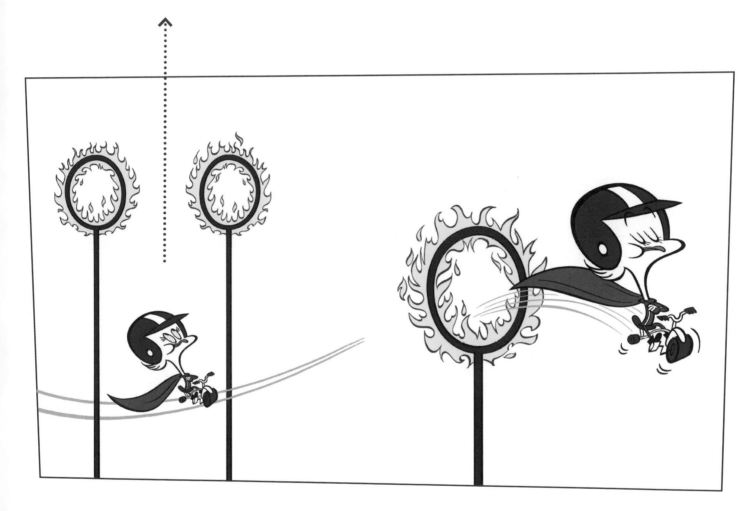

5.

----

through | **between**

CONJUNCTIONS

conjunctions

join up words, phrases, and clauses.

Complete the sentences below with the correct conjunction.

and	but	because	so

1. Plato made a strawberry ......**and**...... banana smoothie.

2. Bearnice was tired .... she went to bed.

3. Bogart was late .... he missed the bus.

4. Oz doesn't like to sing, ... she likes to dance.

PLURALS -S AND -ES

To make a noun plural, you can:
Add -s to most nouns or add -es, if the
noun ends in -s, -ch, -sh, -x, or -z.

Write out these plural nouns.

1. **tree + s =** _trees_

2. **hand + s =** _____

3. **fox + es =** _____

4. **glass + es =** _____

5. **goat + s =** _____

6. **wish + es =** _____

7. **house + s =** _____

8. **beach + es =** _____

IRREGULAR PLURALS

Normally, you add -s or -es to a noun to make it plural.

Some nouns do not follow this rule. These change their spelling.

Circle the word that matches the picture.

1.
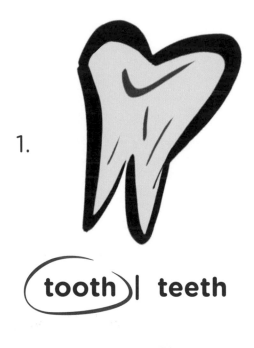

(tooth) | teeth

2.

mice | mouse

3.
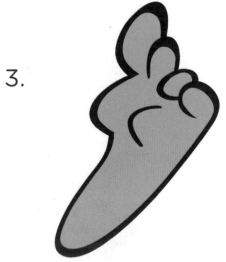

feet | foot

4.

children | child

5.

leaves | leaf

6.

geese | goose

7.

wolf | wolves

Every sentence ends with
a punctuation mark.

 This is a **period**. It comes at the
end of a sentence.

This is a **question mark**. It comes at
the end of a question.

 This is an **exclamation point**.
It comes at the end of a sentence
that shows a strong feeling.

Draw a line to match the
punctuation marks to their names.

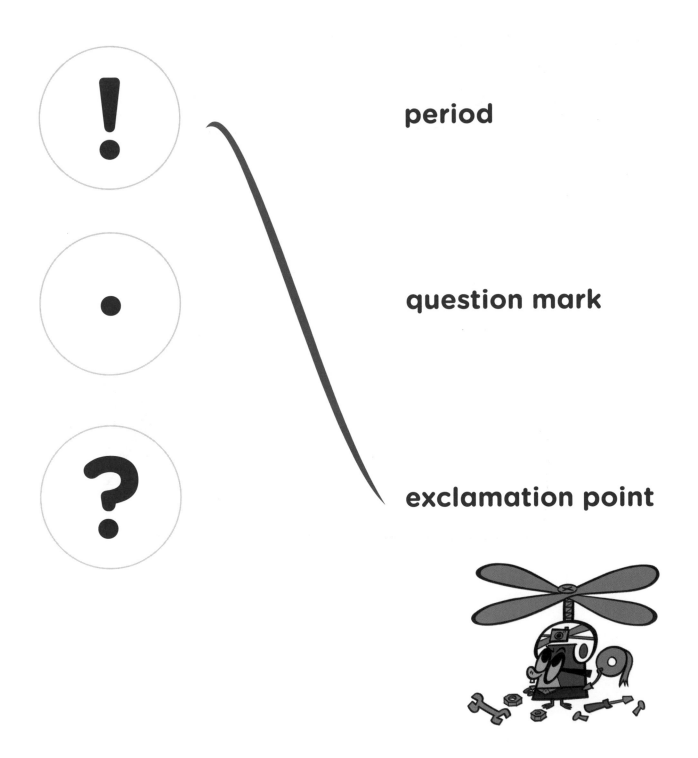

period

question mark

exclamation point

A statement tells something. It ends with a period.

I am hungry.

A question asks something that needs an answer. It ends with a question mark.

When is lunch?

STATEMENTS

Circle the statements.

1 (Oz is a singer.)   Does Oz love to paint?

2 Is Plato a chef?   Plato is a chef.

3 Yin ate her dinner.   What did Yin eat for dinner?

4 When did Bearnice go to bed?   Bearnice went to bed.

5 Did Grit brush his teeth?   Grit brushed his teeth.

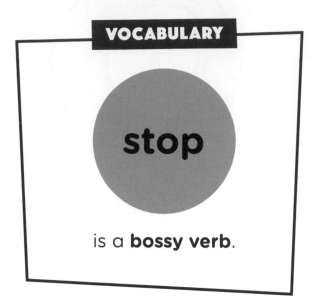

stop

is a **bossy verb**.

Imperatives are bossy verbs—they tell you what to do.

They go at the start of a sentence
to turn it into a command.

Make these sentences bossy!
The first one is done for you.

1. Could you stop drawing on the walls please?

   Stop drawing on the walls! --------------------------------

2. I would like you to make my dinner.

   ----

3. Would you please read me a story?

120

Questions often start with a question word.

Who? To ask about a person.
What? To ask about a thing.
When? To ask about a time.
Where? To ask about a place.
Why? To ask for a reason.

Pick the right question word and write it in the blank.

WORDS

1. _Who_ ate the cake?

   (Who) | When

2. _____ is your birthday?

   When | Why

3. _____ do you live?

   What | Where

4. _____ is fire hot?

   Why | Who

5. _____ is your new teacher?

   Who | When

6. _____ is in your bag?

   Why | What

HIGH-FREQUENCY WORDS

HIGH- FREQUENCY WORDS

from

it's

just

don't

it's

day

day

just

Use the paint by words chart to complete the picture
and find the hidden words. Use crayons, pencils, or paint!

BLUE just

RED from

GREEN day

ORANGE it's

YELLOW don't

When you've found
them all, color the
rest of the picture.

BROWN
so

ORANGE
saw

YELLOW
how

PINK
her

GREEN
do

BLACK
by

MATH CONCEPTS & VOCABULARY

EVEN NUMBERS

VOCABULARY

even

possible to split
into twos

How many gloves? Count the even number of gloves and write it in the blank.

1.

_____2_____

_____two_____

2.

_____

_____

3.

_____

_____

4.

_____

_____

5.

_____

_____

128

ODD NUMBERS

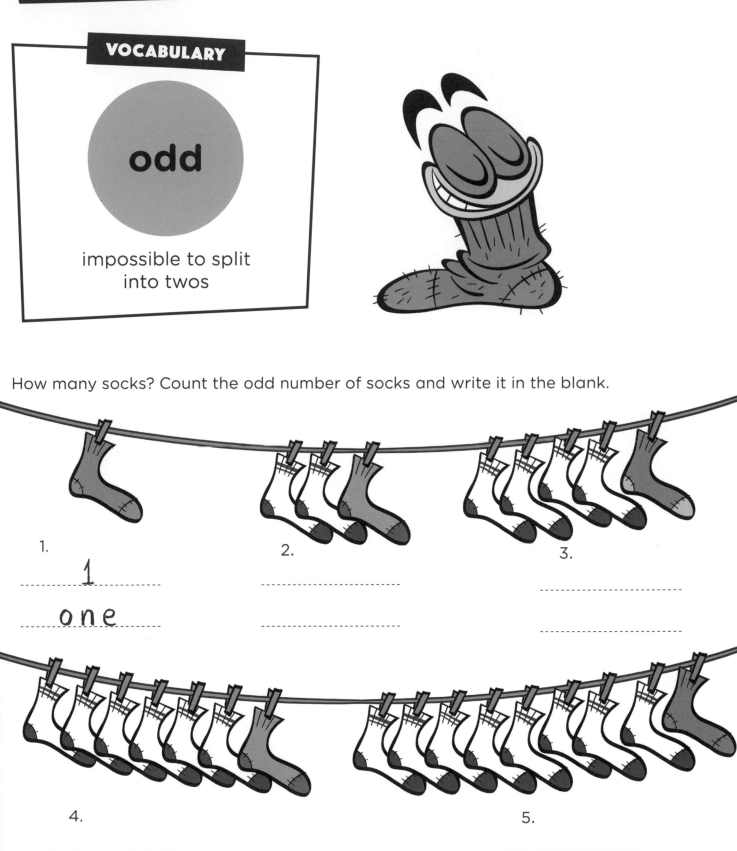

How many socks? Count the odd number of socks and write it in the blank.

1.
___1___

___one___

2.
_____

_____

3.
_____

_____

4.
_____

_____

5.
_____

_____

VOCABULARY

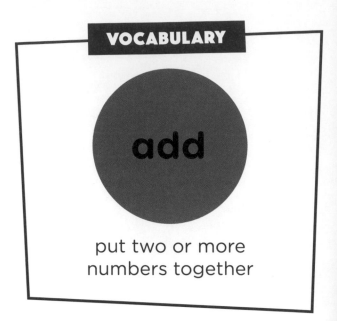

add

put two or more
numbers together

Add up the cookies! Write your answers in the blanks.

one plus one equals...

1.  1 + 1 = 2

two plus two equals...

2.  +  =

four plus four equals...

3.  +  =

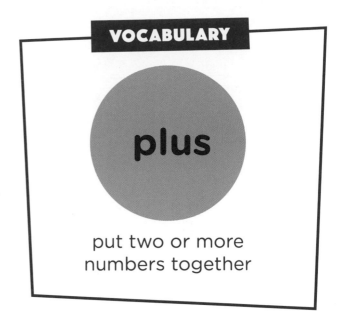

4.   A cat has five toes on its front paws and four toes on its back paws. Add them up!

$5 + 5 + 4 + 4 =$ _18_

5.   A platypus has five toes on each of its four webbed feet. Add them up!

$5 + 5 + 5 + 5 =$ _____

6.   An ostrich has two toes on each of its two feet. Add them up!

2 + 2 = _____

7.   A hippo has four toes on each of its four feet. Add them up!

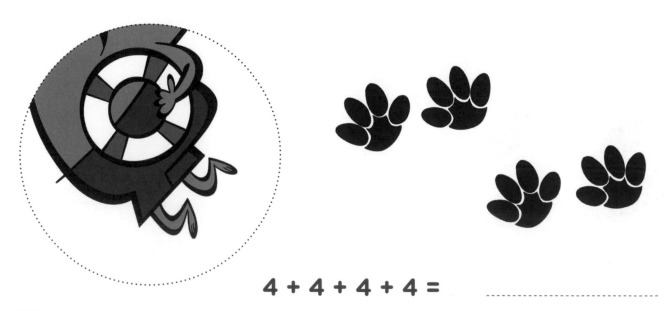

4 + 4 + 4 + 4 = _____

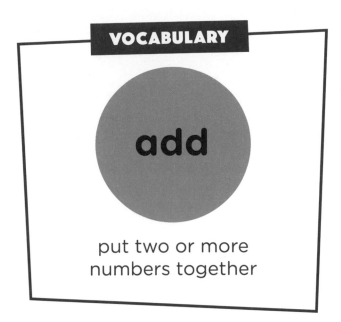
8. A giraffe has two toes on each of its four feet. Add them up!

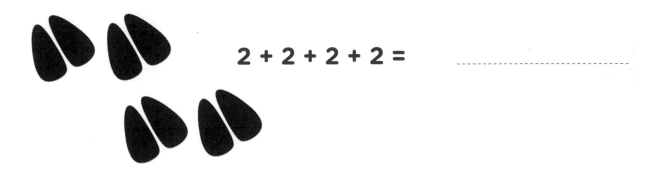

$2 + 2 + 2 + 2 =$ _____

9. And finally, how many toes do worms have?

_____

subtract or minus

take a number away from another

Subtract the cookies! Write your answers in the blanks.

two minus one equals...

1.  2 − 1 = 1

four minus two equals...

2.  −  =

eight minus four equals...

3.  −  =

VOCABULARY

number bond

a pair of numbers that add up to another number

Use the stack of tires to help you complete the number bonds.

1. _____1_____ + _____9_____ = 10

2. _____ + _____ = 10

3. _____ + _____ = 10

4. _____ + _____ = 10

5. _____ + _____ = 10

SKIP COUNTING BY TWOS

counting in twos

Count the cheeks full of cookies! Write the numbers in the blanks.

1.

_____ 2 _____

_____ two _____

3.

_____

_____

2.

_____

_____

4.

_____

_____

5.

_____

_____

Keep going!

6.

12
twelve

8.

7.

9.

10.

counting in fives

There are five doughnuts in each box. Write how many doughnuts Plato eats in the blanks!

1. <u>5</u>
    five

2.

------

3. ------

    ------

4. ------

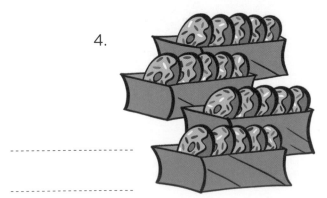

5.

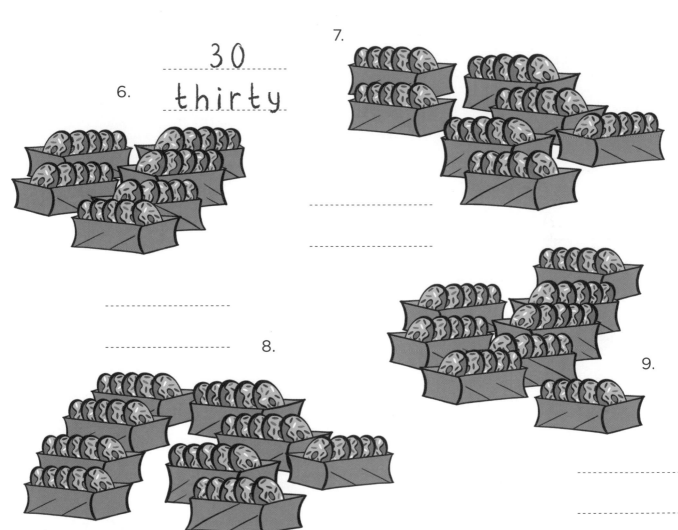

6.
30
thirty

7.

8.

9.

counting in tens

There are 10 bees in each family. How many bees are in each swarm?
Write the numbers in the blanks.

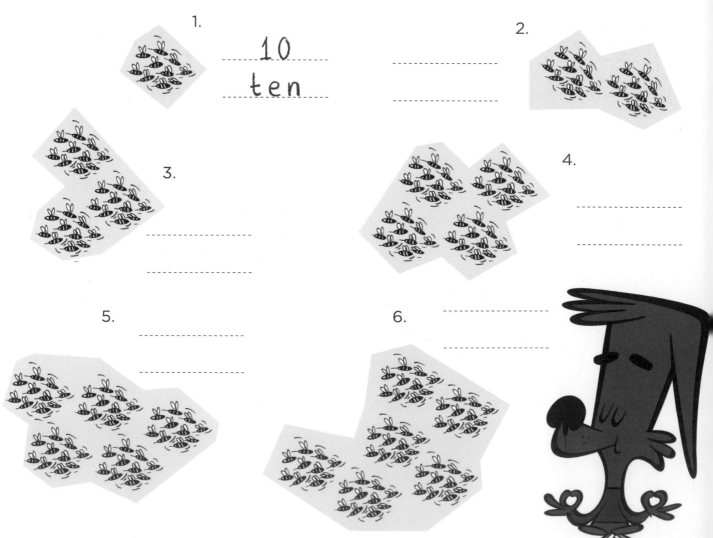

1. _____10_____
_____ten_____

2. _____

3. _____
_____

4. _____
_____

5. _____
_____

6. _____
_____

I can't sleep!

Help Shang High fall
asleep by counting the sheep.

Write the number words in the blanks.

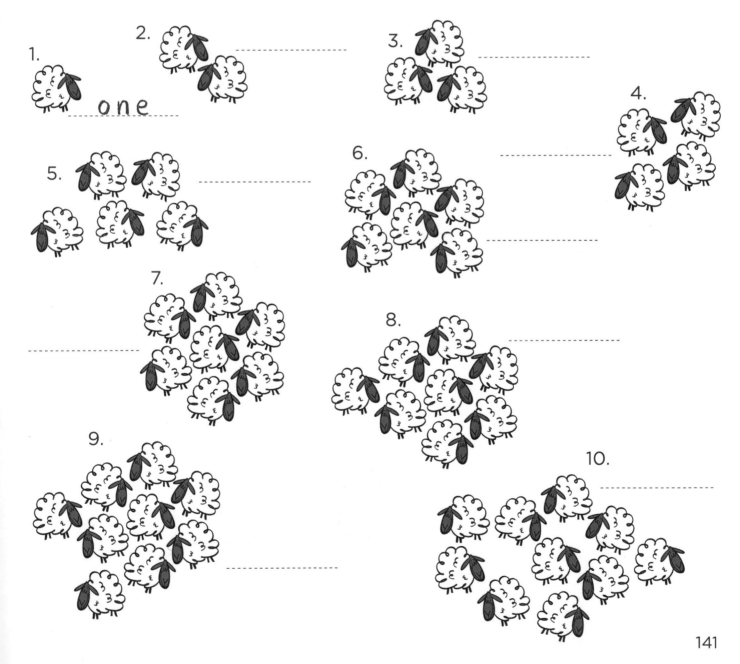

1.

_____ o n e _____

2. _____

3. _____

4. _____

5. _____

6. _____

7. _____

8. _____

9. _____

10. _____

MEASURING IN CENTIMETERS

10 mm
1 cm

25 mm
2.5 cm

150 mm
15 cm

Use your hot dog ruler to measure these things in your kitchen in centimeters!

a carrot

a jar

a fork

----
cm

----
cm

----
cm

MEASURING IN FEET

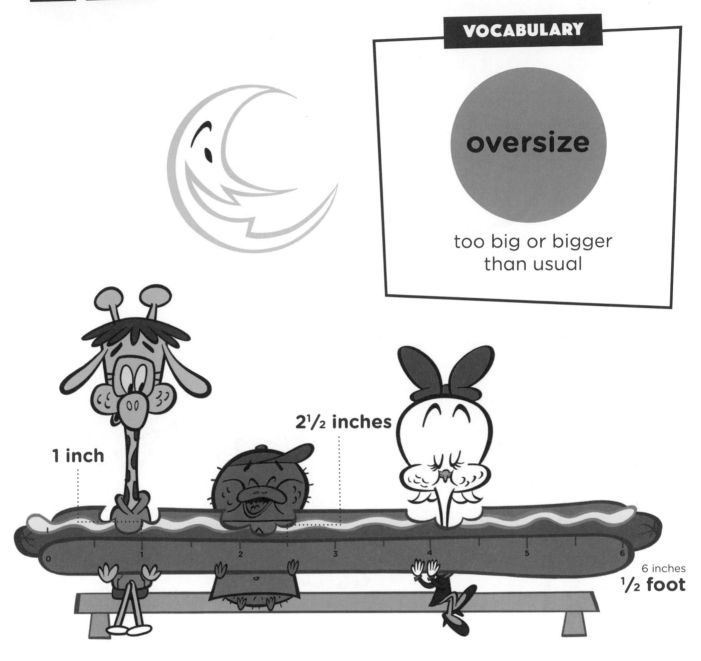

VOCABULARY

oversize

too big or bigger than usual

1 inch

2½ inches

6 inches
½ foot

Now use your hot dog ruler to measure these things in inches!

a glass

----
inches

a slice of bread

----
inches

MEASURING HEIGHT

Not to scale

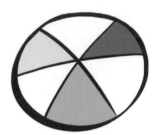

How many feet tall is the wave that Armie is surfing?

50 ft

45 ft

40 ft

35 ft

30 ft

25 ft

20 ft

15 ft

10 ft

meter

a unit of measurement
that equals
100 centimeters

How many meters tall is the wave that Armie is surfing?

50 m

45 m

40 m

35 m

30 m

25 m

20 m

15 m

10 m

UNDERSTANDING BAR CHARTS

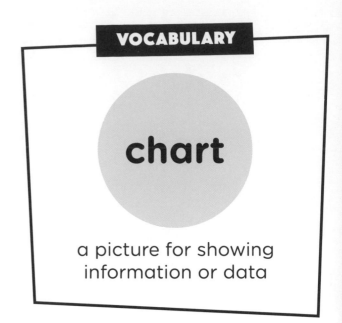

How many glasses of water should each age group drink per day?
Read the chart and write the numbers in the blanks!

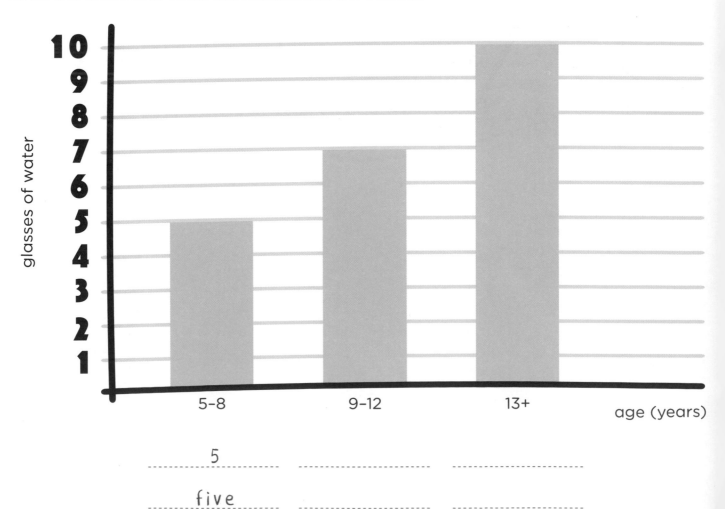

glasses of water

10
9
8
7
6
5
4
3
2
1

5-8   9-12   13+   age (years)

5

five

3D SHAPES

3D shapes

three dimensional—solid!

Can you match the 3D shapes to the objects?
Draw a line with your pencil!

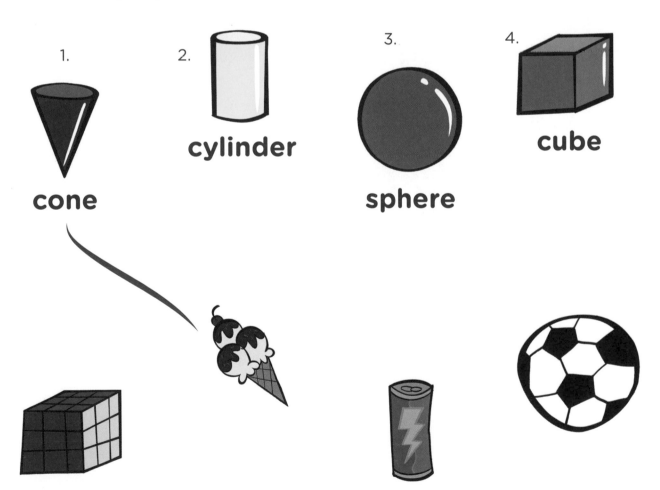

1.

cone

2.

cylinder

3.

sphere

4.

cube

VOCABULARY

money

what you use to buy stuff

PLATO'S

TACOS

Look at today's menu.
Write down how much
it will cost to order:

TODAY'S MENU

10 tacos

5 kiwi juice

10 burritos

2 doughnut

5 guacamole

1. **One taco and one kiwi juice?**

   $15

   fifteen dollars

2. **Two doughnuts?**

3. **Two burritos and one guacamole?**

4. **One of everything on the menu?**

148

YOUR TEETH FOR **2 MINUTES**

How long is Grit brushing his teeth for?
Write your answers in the blanks!

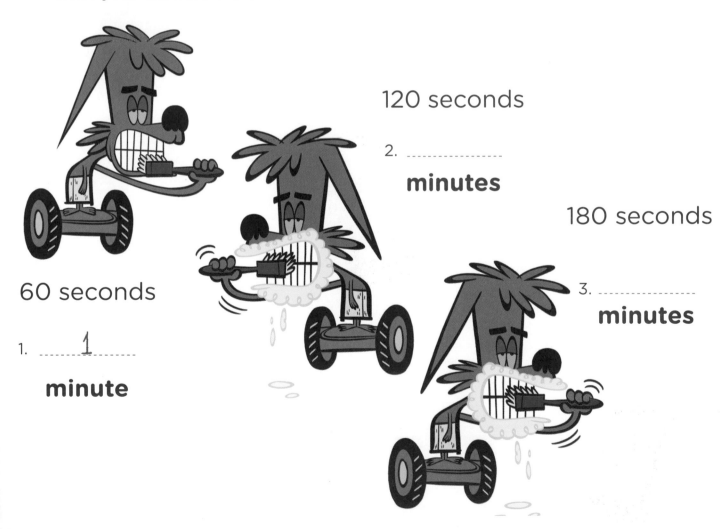

120 seconds

2. _____ **minutes**

180 seconds

3. _____ **minutes**

60 seconds

1. _____1_____ **minute**

ADDING UP:
MINUTES & HOURS

screen time

the amount of time you spend looking at a device

Ask everyone in your family how long they think they spend looking at devices every day.

Name	Time looking at devices (hours and minutes)
....	....
....	....
....	....
....	....
....	....
....	....

Now add them up! In total, how long does your family spend looking at screens?

.... **hours**

.... **minutes**

TELLING TIME

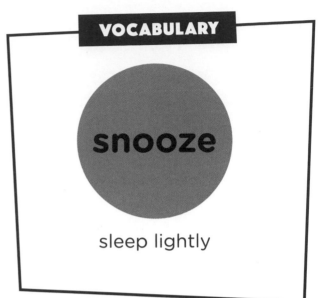

VOCABULARY

snooze

sleep lightly

Grit forgot to set his alarm clock! Look at the clocks and write the times.

1.

s e v e n o'clock

7:00

2.

_____ **o'clock**

3.

_____ **o'clock**

4.

_____ **o'clock**

5.

_____ **o'clock**

VOCABULARY

drowsy

when you feel like you are about to fall asleep

Looks like it's time for Yin and Yang's nap! Look at the clocks and write the times.

6.

half past two **o'clock**

2:30

7.

_____ **o'clock**

_____

8.

_____ **o'clock**

_____

9.

_____ **o'clock**

_____

10.

_____ **o'clock**

_____

exhausted

when you are very tired
and worn out

How late did Shang High go to bed? He's exhausted!
Look at the clocks and write the times.

11.

half past eleven **o'clock**

11:30

13.

_____ **o'clock**

12.

_____ **o'clock**

14.

_____ **o'clock**

15.

_____ **o'clock**

153

LISTENING, SPEAKING, CREATING

ALL ABOUT ME-MOJI

HI! MY NAME IS

_____

Draw your me-moji:

I AM

_____

YEARS OLD

THIS IS MY FAMILY

Circle a me-moji that shows how you feel.

MY FRIENDS ARE

_____

_____

_____

_____

HAPPY

CONFUSED

SAD

SILLY

MISCHIEVOUS

MY FAVORITE:

3D — lite

PRINTER

_____ food

_____ color

_____ sport

_____ book

_____ video game

_____ TV show

If I could have any pet in the world, it would be a...

_____

CAUSE & EFFECT

Draw what you think will happen as a result of the first image.
Write a sentence to show what happened under both images.

CAUSE:

What happened first?

- -

- -

EFFECT:

What happened as a result?

Cause and effect show how two events are related.
The second event (effect) happens as a result of
the first event (cause).

CAUSE & EFFECT

Draw what you think will happen as a result of the first image.
Write a sentence to show what happened under both images.

CAUSE:

What happened first?

EFFECT:

What happened as a result?

Cause and effect show how two events are related. The second event (effect) happens as a result of the first event (cause).

CAUSE & EFFECT

Draw what you think happened first.
Write a sentence to show what happened under both images.

What happened first?

162

What happened as a result?

Cause and effect show how two events are related.
The second event (effect) happens as a result of
the first event (cause).

SEQUENCING

Write **1** in the circle to show what happened **first**. Write **2** in the circle to show what happened **next**. Write **3** in the circle to show what happened **last**. Write a sentence next to each image to explain what is happening.

Color in the picture!

NOTHING IS BEYOND YOUR REACH.

VOCABULARY

challenge

something that is difficult to do or finish

1. Trace the words.

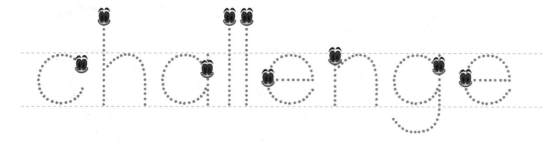

challenge

2. Try it out. Start with Bogart's emoji.

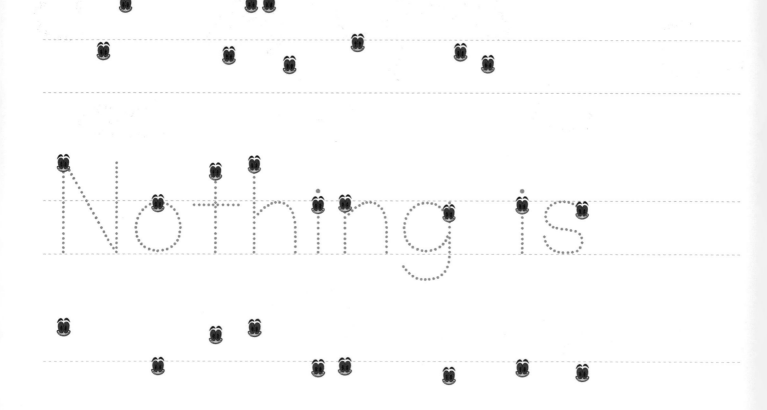

Nothing is

beyond

your

reach.

Color in the picture!

REMEMBER, FEELINGS COME AND GO.

1. Trace the words.

2. Try it out. Start with Bogart's emoji.

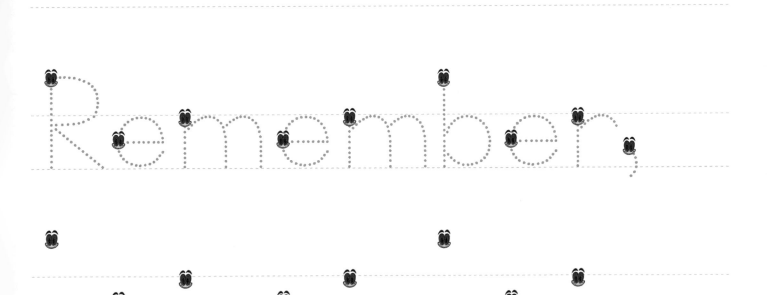

feelings

come

and go.

Color in the picture!

COLLECT MEMORIES, NOT THINGS.

VOCABULARY

friends

people who get along
well and love each other

1. Trace the words.

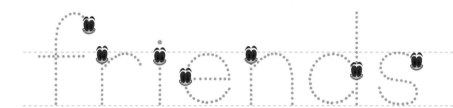

2. Try it out. Start with Bogart's emoji.

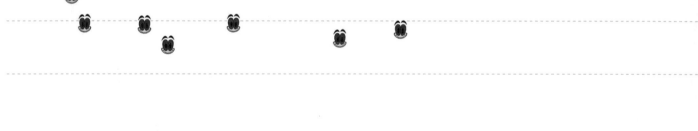

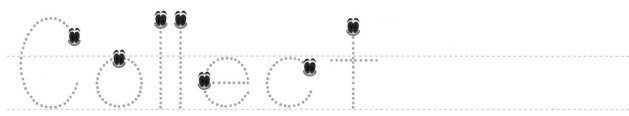

174

memories

not

things.

TEDDY Talks: 3D PRINTING

Teddy Talks are about creating something new and sharing it with the world!

VOCABULARY

design

plan to make something

Oz is using a 3D printer to make a new teddy bear. A 3D printer prints thousands of tiny slices of plastic that fit together like a puzzle. Then it stacks these slices like pancakes to make a solid object like a teddy bear!

Now that you have all the answers,
give a Teddy Talk about them!

1. What is a 3D printer?

2. How does it work?

3. What would you make in a printer?

1. Write your notes here.

2. Draw a picture to show someone.

TEDDY Talks:
HOW TO TIE YOUR SHOES

Teddy Talks are about creating something new and sharing it with the world!

VOCABULARY

understand

know how or why something works

Look at the instructions for how to tie your shoes in five easy steps.
Make sure you remember them all!

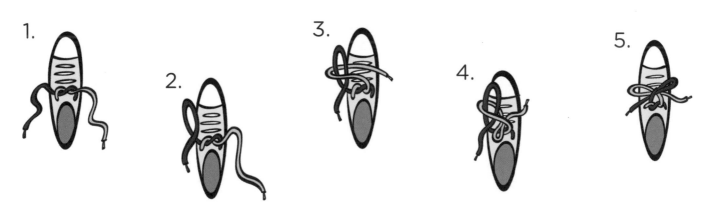

1.

2.

3.

4.

5.

Now give a Teddy Talk to your family and friends,
explaining how to tie your shoes!

1. What are shoes?

2. Why do we need to tie them?

3. What's the first step?

4. What's the final step?

1. Write your notes here.

TEDDY Talks:

DESIGN YOUR OWN HOVERBOARD

VOCABULARY

hoverboard

a mode of transportation you stand on that floats above the ground

What's even more exciting than a scooter? A hoverboard! Design yours on the next page and make a list of some of its best features.

1. Design your own hoverboard here.

2. What are your hoverboard's best features?

ANSWER KEY

PAGE 19

rain—L

cat—S

paint—L

egg—S

feet—L

bed—S

night—L

pig—S

milk—S

mop—S

goat—L

boat—L

duck—S

boot—L

sun—S

PAGE 20

1. paint—long vowel

2. cat—short vowel

3. rain—long vowel

4. ant—short vowel

PAGE 21

1. sheep—long vowel

2. feet—long vowel

3. nest—short vowel

4. red—short vowel

PAGE 22

1. fish—short vowel

2. ring—short vowel

3. night—long vowel

4. light—long vowel

PAGE 23

1. toad—long vowel

2. box—short vowel

3. toast—long vowel

4. dog—short vowel

PAGE 24

1. sun—short vowel

2. food—long vowel

3. shampoo—long vowel

4. bug—short vowel

PAGE 25

Short vowels: **bag milk frog ant sun**
Long vowels: **soap room high sail bee**

PAGE 36–37

Short vowels: **map hat man plum duck**
Long vowels: **feet coin night tree join**

Short vowels: **hot mop stuck cap kit**
Long vowels: **point moon tooth queen tail**

PAGE 49–51

Page 49
1. **cape**
2. **cane**

Page 50
3. **kite**
4. **robe**

Page 51
5. **cube**
6. **tape**
7. **cute**
8. **hate**

PAGE 52–54

1. t**oa**d
2. b**ea**ch
3. s**ai**l
4. c**oa**t
5. sw**ee**t
6. p**ea**s

PAGE 55–56

1. em**ai**l
2. b**ee**
3. wh**ee**l
4. b**oa**t
5. br**ai**n
6. r**ea**d
7. g**oa**t
8. ti**e**

PAGE 58–59

1. t**oy**
2. s**oi**l
3. j**oy**
4. t**oi**let
5. h**ow**l
6. cl**ou**d
7. **ow**l
8. fl**ow**er

PAGE 60

9. sn**ow**
10. b**oi**l
11. m**ou**se
12. ann**oy**

PAGE 62–63

1. n**ur**se
2. sh**ar**k
3. th**ir**sty
4. h**ur**t
5. t**ur**tle
6. g**er**ms

1. j**ar**
2. h**or**se
3. b**ur**ger
4. popc**or**n
5. sh**ir**t
6. **ar**t

PAGE 64-65

1. **cr**ab
2. **cl**ock
3. **pl**anet
4. **sc**arf
5. **st**airs
6. **fl**ower
7. **sn**ake
8. **dr**ess

PAGE 66-67

1. **sw**ing
2. **st**ar
3. **sn**ow
4. **sl**ed
5. **sc**ale
6. **cr**own

PAGE 68-69

1. po**nd**
2. ba**nk**
3. pai**nt**
4. toa**st**
5. la**mp**
6. ne**st**
7. e**lf**
8. ha**nd**

PAGE 70-71

1. sta**mp**
2. sa**nd**
3. te**nt**
4. go**lf**
5. gi**ft**
6. toa**st**

PAGE 72

1. sing = ring
2. fell = bell
3. rock = sock
4. wall = ball
5. look = book

PAGE 73

1. **wash**
2. **bag**
3. **pot**
4. **star**
5. **lock**

PAGE 74-75

scream

head

bed

PAGE 76-77

1. r**ing**
2. l**ung**
3. s**ing**
4. k**ing**
5. w**ing**
6. d**ung**
7. sw**ing**
8. b**ang**
9. st**ing**
10. str**ong**

PAGE 80-81

Not real words:
1. gilk
4. spait
5. freeg
14. bink

PAGE 84-85

Not real words:
4. whuck
5. glane
7. gife
11. feal
12. roink

PAGE 92

huge
giant
enormous
gargantuan
colossal

PAGE 95

delighted
overjoyed
ecstatic

PAGE 96-97

1. Monday
2. Tuesday
3. Wednesday
4. Thursday
5. Friday
6. Saturday
7. Sunday

PAGE 98-99

January
February
March
April
May
June

July
August
September
October
November
December

PAGE 100

1. blueberry
2. coconut
3. grape
4. lemon
5. mint
6. orange
7. strawberry
8. vanilla

PAGE 101

1. purple
2. yellow
3. red
4. green
5. blue
6. pink
7. white

PAGE 102

1. The bells ring. =
   She is wearing a ring. =

2. I hit the ball with my bat. =
   The bat can fly. =

PAGE 103

3. He is a fan of sports! =
   The fan kept them cool. =

4. He has a cold. =
   It is cold outside. =

5. She waves with both arms. =
   The ocean waves are strong. =

PAGE 106–108

Verbs: sit, jump, taste, be, think, draw

Nouns: scarf, tree, Oz, house, paint, beach

Adjectives: loud, quiet, tired, blue, hot, frozen

PAGE 109

1. swim

2. kick

3. sleep

4. read

PAGE 110–111

1. over
2. under
3. around
4. between
5. through

PAGE 112

1. and

2. so

3. because

4. but

PAGE 113

1. trees
2. hands
3. foxes
4. glasses
5. goats
6. wishes
7. houses
8. beaches

PAGE 114–115

1. tooth
2. mice
3. foot
4. child
5. leaves
6. goose
7. wolf

PAGE 117

! exclamation mark

? question mark

. period or full stop

PAGE 119

1. Oz is a singer.

2. Plato is a chef.

3. Yin ate her dinner.

4. Bearnice went to bed.

5. Grit brushed his teeth.

PAGE 120

1. Stop drawing on the walls!

2. Make my dinner!

3. Read me a story!

PAGE 121

1. **Who** ate the cake?

2. **When** is your birthday?

3. **Where** do you live?

4. **Why** is fire hot?

5. **Who** is your new teacher?

6. **What** is in your bag?

PAGE 128–129

1. 2, two
2. 4, four
3. 6, six
4. 8, eight
5. 10, ten

1. 1, one
2. 3, three
3. 5, five
4. 7, seven
5. 9, nine

PAGE 130–133

1. 1 + 1 = 2

2. 2 + 2 = 4

3. 4 + 4 = 8

4. 18

5. 20

6. 4

7. 16

8. 8

9. 0

PAGE 134

1. 2 - 1 = 1

2. 4 - 2 = 2

3. 8 - 4 = 4

PAGE 135

1. 1 + 9 = 10

2. 4 + 6 = 10

3. 5 + 5 = 10

4. 3 + 7 = 10

5. 2 + 8 = 10

PAGE 136-137

1. 2, two
2. 4, four
3. 6, six
4. 8, eight
5. 10, ten
6. 12, twelve
7. 14, fourteen
8. 16, sixteen
9. 18, eighteen
10. 20, twenty

PAGE 138-139

1. 5, five
2. 10, ten
3. 15, fifteen
4. 20, twenty
5. 25, twenty-five
6. 30, thirty
7. 35, thirty-five
8. 40, forty
9. 45, forty-five

PAGE 140

1. 10, ten
2. 20, twenty
3. 30, thirty
4. 40, forty
5. 50, fifty
6. 60, sixty

PAGE 141

1. 1, one
2. 2, two
3. 3, three
4. 4, four
5. 5, five
6. 6, six
7. 7, seven
8. 8, eight
9. 9, nine
10. 10, ten

PAGE 144-145

1. 35 ft
2. 30 m

PAGE 146

1. 5, five
2. 7, seven
3. 10, ten

PAGE 147

 =

 =

 =

 =

PAGE 148

1. $15, fifteen dollars
2. $4, four dollars
3. $25, twenty-five dollars
4. $32, thirty-two dollars

PAGE 149

1. 1 minute

2. 2 minutes

3. 3 minutes

PAGE 151

1. seven, 7:00
2. nine, 9:00
3. ten, 10:00
4. eight, 8:00
5. twelve, 12:00

PAGE 152

6. half past two, 2:30
7. half past eight, 8:30
8. half past seven, 7:30
9. half past twelve, 12:30
10. half past six, 6:30

PAGE 153

11. half past eleven, 11:30
12. half past ten, 10:30
13. nine, 9:00
14. ten, 10:00
15. one, 1:00

PAGE 164

3

1

2

PAGE 165

2

1

3

PAGE 166

3

1

2

MEET THE
MRS WORDSMITH TEAM

Editor-in-Chief
Sofia Fenichell

Associate Creative Director
Lady San Pedro

Art Director
Craig Kellman

Writers

Tatiana Barnes

Mark Holland
Sawyer Eaton

Amelia Mehra

Researcher
Eleni Savva

Lexicographer
Ian Brookes

Designers

Suzanne Bullat
James Sales

Fabrice Gourdel
James Webb
Holly Jones

Caroline Henriksen
Jess Macadam

Producers
Eva Schumacher Payne
Leon Welters

Academic Advisors
Emma Madden
Prof. Susan Neuman

Project Managers
Senior Editor Helen Murray
Design Manager Sunita Gahir

Senior Production Editor Jennifer Murray
US Editor Kayla Dugger
Senior Production Controller Louise Minihane
Publishing Director Mark Searle

DK Delhi
DTP Designers Satish Gaur and Rohit Rojal
Senior DTP Designer Pushpak Tyagi
Pre-production Manager Sunil Sharma
Managing Art Editor Romi Chakraborty

DK would like to thank Anna Formanek for design assistance,
and Roohi Sehgal, Lisa Stock, and Julia March for
editorial assistance.

First American Edition, 2022
Published in the United States by DK Publishing
1745 Broadway, 20th Floor, New York, NY 10019

Variations of this content are available as
printable worksheets at mrswordsmith.com
24 25 26 10 9 8 7 6 5 4 3
005–325947–Jan/2022

A catalog record for this book
is available from the Library of Congress.
ISBN 978-0-7440-5153-7

Printed and bound in Malaysia

www.dk.com

mrswordsmith.com

For the curious

The building blocks of reading

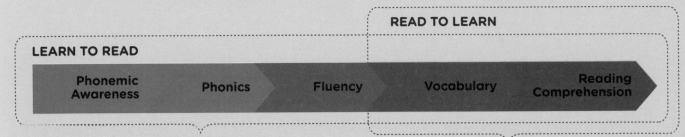

READ TO LEARN

LEARN TO READ

| Phonemic Awareness | Phonics | Fluency | Vocabulary | Reading Comprehension |

Readiculous App
App Store & Google Play

Word Tag App
App Store & Google Play

OUR JOB IS TO INCREASE YOUR CHILD'S READING AGE

This book adheres to the science of reading. Our research-backed learning helps children progress through phonemic awareness, phonics, fluency, vocabulary, and reading comprehension.